Motivate Black Boys:

How to Prepare Your Sons for Careers in Science, Technology, Engineering and Mathematics

Gerald A. Moore Sr.

ISBN: 9781691327935

Published by Gerald Moore 360 LLC PO Box 1691 44715 Prentice Drive, Dulles, VA 20101

Cover design by: Micheal Shaw, Icon Photographic

Edited by: Critique Editing Services, LLC

Dedication

I would like to dedicate this book in loving memory of my parents, Gerald John Henry Moore and Carolyn Elaine Burno-Moore, for without them nothing that I have accomplished in life would have been possible. Thank you for your loving support as I was finding my way as a young boy maturing into a man.

To my mother, though your life on this earth was short, you touched so many people and for your goodness, I receive much grace because, "that's Carolyn's son." Thank you, Mom for always believing in me and not being afraid to tell me when you thought I was wrong. The most important thing you've ever said to me still rings clear to this day, and I teach it to others. You said, "You can't fault people for their shortcomings, but you can help them." It's these words that have placed me in a mindset to be of service to others; therefore, you live through me. Love You.

To my dad, you were always a man's man who loved his family and gave me the belief that I could do anything. Thank you for not sparing the rod, for I would not be the man that I am today. Through your greatness, wisdom and your flaws, I am always guided by your light. While the quote, “Do as I say and not as I do” is still a flawed concept that I did not adopt, I get your intent and it keeps me on the right path. There is nowhere that I go, North or South, that I don’t hear, “There go John Henry.” You live on through me and I represent you well. I miss you, old man.

Acknowledgements

I would like to thank my children: Gerald Jr., Andrea, Lauren, Jada and Jordan Moore, and their mom Aisha. You all keep me grinding daily. I am extremely proud of you all. Keep working hard.

To all of my immediate and extended family, the Moores, Burnos, and the Solomons, thank you. To all my brothers: PFG Crew, Breck Street Massive and my day ones, Nuff Respect.

Special thanks to Mr. Micheal Shaw for letting me know that I was doing the world a disservice for not sharing my gifts and for being my sounding board for my crazy ideas, also for being my photographer, graphic designer, friend and Emcee.

Thanks to my editor Karen Rodgers of Critique Editing Services, who has been a gem during this process.

Super Special Thanks to Rachelle Julmice for believing in me; your support is everything. You encourage me daily and I'm grateful. I am truly in anticipation of our future together and my words don't clearly express my feelings, therefore my loving actions will have to suffice.

Love Ya. #National Harbor

Contents

Foreword

Black young men face a myriad of challenges and threats in America today. From police brutality, educational deficits, mass incarceration, abject poverty, and structural racism, there is no shortage of landmines waiting to destroy our young kings' futures. As a black father, husband, and brother, I am deeply concerned with the state of our world and the tactical threats that face our young men. Within my caution and concern, there is still great hope that we can navigate a new course for the successful development of black male youth. Coach Moore is a bright light in this dimly lit space. His story is one of trial and triumph. Coming from the toughest neighborhoods in Rochester, NY, he has personally lived the life that many of our young brothers walk daily.

Gerald has been a business partner, friend, and life-transformational coach of mine for more than twenty-five years. I have seen him grow and redefine his strategies and approach and through tests and testimony. He has worked with and inspired black young men at every level for more than thirty years, and his approach is proven. From school age to college and pro athletes, his influence and compassion cannot be understated. He loves to inspire and bring hope to all that he encounters.

Once you have interacted with Coach Moore, you will know that he is the real deal. Simply put, Gerald has a gift for uplifting people and a special understanding of what is uniquely necessary to reach young black men at their adolescence. It is my distinct honor to have a chance to see Gerald expand his reach and share his talents within this new chapter of his life. As you read his story and reflect on his experiences be reminded that the work is real, and we all have a responsibility to *Motivate Black Boys*.

Micheal Shaw

Founder, Team Jenny Bean

Introduction

I was the typical black boy growing up in the hood. I just happened to figure out how to beat the system and became an engineer against all odds.

I stole from the corner store. I cursed like a sailor behind my parents' back. I was mischievous, devious and many more less than positive adjectives than I would like to admit. I also probably did way more dirt than the average black boy in my neighborhood. At the same time, I was hardworking, intelligent, outgoing and respectful to those I respected.

I'm a product of the '80s and '90s Hip Hop culture, which was supposed to have been dead, said the adults when I was a teenager. But Hip Hop culture today runs the world. The unfortunate part of that is the Hip Hop culture that challenged me to be great is the same culture pushing young black males to stay dumb, drunk, high and abusive to women. Public Enemy told me to "Fight the Power," and I did just that. With that said, like most kids today, I still love, live and breathe the culture, which is one of rebellion, breaking the rules and doing things your way.

It's nothing new that if you ask most black boys what they're going to do when they grow up, the answer will be the same as mine was 35 years ago: "I'm going to make the NBA, NFL or be a rap star." But unlike most black boys, I actually had the drive and potential to make it happen, yet I failed.

I was locally known and recognized in my city for my ability to play football and basketball. I was a beast in football all through Pop Warner. I won many little league championships and was an All Greater Rochester high school player in Upstate New York. My room looked like the Hall of Fame with all of the MVP and All-Star trophies I had earned. If I would have been more obedient and done my schoolwork, I would have gotten a full college scholarship and would not still be paying off those damn student loans, but that's a topic for another book.

I fell in love with the Hip Hop Deejays and music production when I was about 12 years old, and that's still a passion of mine today. The highlight of my Hip Hop career came when a good friend of mine, Mike Shaw, who I met in high school formed a group called "Arctic Circle." We opened for the Fugees on their first tour in our hometown, and Lauren Hill told me I was "Hot." Their manager asked if we could tour with them and seeing how Wyclef and Lauren blew up after that, I always wonder if I had blown my opportunity to be a rap star. But I was a freshman in college with a child that I had sole custody of at that point and had begun to make better life choices. I had a clear understanding that whatever I did or did not accomplish would have a direct impact on the future of my son. But you never know though, Jay-Z is older than me and he is still getting it done, so maybe I still have an album in me.

One of my flaws growing up was I loved to fight. I was suspended from middle school more times than I care to discuss. I blame my dad for that as I wanted to be tough like him. My dad took no shit, for lack of better words, and was well respected in my neighborhood. He stood about 6'3" and was diesel—the slang at the time for muscular.

At the end of my 8th-grade year, I got into a fight and got expelled from the Rochester City School District, which meant I would have to go to an alternative high school. That summer, I beat up another kid in the neighborhood pretty bad and ended up in the local Scared Straight Program. If you are unfamiliar, lookup "Scared Straight" on Netflix. Having to spend a day in the stinking county jail with career criminals spitting on me as they yelled was my turning point, getting me off the path of juvenile delinquency. I knew that I didn't want to end up in prison, mainly because I knew I couldn't make the NFL from jail. I had big dreams for my life.

When school started that September, I probably received one of the biggest blessings of my life. I was attending my long-term suspension hearing with my mother and the school administrator was going down my rap sheet of school transgressions and making the recommendation for me to attend an alternative school. Fortunately for me, this was one of the first hearings of the school year, and the superintendent of schools was in the meeting. He asked the question, "Has anyone reviewed Mr. Moore's New York State standardized test record?" The room got dead silent. The school administrator said that he had not. The superintendent proceeded to state that I scored at 12th-grade, 8th month level in reading and math, which meant I had virtually tested out of high school by the end of 8th grade. He then said that I could choose any school in the city to go to outside of my home district. I decided to go to Edison Technical Occupational Center, a vocational high school, which is where I received my diploma.

Looking back on my childhood, I realize I was very fortunate. I came from a good two-parent dysfunctional home. Don't get it twisted when I use the word "dysfunctional." My parents were very hardworking, and my home life was stable. I grew up in the same house until I went off to college. But my father smoked weed and drank a 40oz. malt liquor after work almost every day of my home life that I can remember. My mother worked hard and was the eldest of nine, and I did not understand the stress and pressure of that until I was an adult and she was dead. There were a couple of separations along the way, but in hindsight, I had it better than most young black boys in my neighborhood.

Even though I came from a household with structure and was disciplined for doing wrong, I still was on the verge of becoming a product of my environment. I was one of those boys who needed to learn the hard way, but I was very fortunate that my parents did not give up on me even though I was a rebel.

I would say that my parents did an awesome job raising my sisters and me, but despite their efforts to rear us in the way that we should go, there are also other outside influences that come into play that are beyond a parent's control. I became an engineer more because of what my parents did right than what they could have done better, which is why I am writing this book.

I would say that most parents of black boys, especially the mothers, envision great futures for them. Then somewhere down the road, those dreams and aspirations get derailed. I am not an aberration, but the norm for black boys. Most are extraordinarily talented and intellectually gifted. Unfortunately, we have seen many of those same gifts lead more black men to jail than to prosperous careers, such as engineers. What's needed is the right type of guidance before the streets capture their attention.

From my perspective, having the opportunity to coach youth sports for over 25 years, Black boys are nurtured by their mothers, and they are very eager to please until around the age of 10. At that point there seems to be an inexplicable lack of motivation. There are a lot of reasons for this that go beyond the context of this book. I am also not a psychologist, nor have I done a massive, intense documented study on black boys. My knowledge comes from my personal experience from being that black boy, having two sons of my own and coaching and mentoring hundreds of black boys over the years.

What you will find in this book are tools and strategies I've gained through my experience that will help you to guide and prepare black boys to fill the science, technology, engineering and mathematics (STEM) field and Digital skills talent gap where researchers predict millions of jobs will remain unfilled and trillions of dollars in unrealized revenues by 2030.

Chapter 1: Exposing Black Boys to High Tech and STEM Careers

For a long time I didn't know that my children had no clue what I did for a living. They knew that I was an engineer, but I took for granted that they knew what that meant.

It wasn't until I agreed to go to my son's school for a career day presentation that I realized he had no clue what I did.

On the ride home he said, "Dad, I didn't know you did that," and I responded, "You knew I was an engineer," at which time he replied, "You just sit at your computer doing nothing." I laughed, as I thought about it more from his perspective, that I did nothing. Because at the time a lot of what I did was mental exercises and nothing very tangible or something you could explain to an 8 or 9 year-old. But what I realized was that I needed to expose not only my children, but more importantly, black boys in general to me as an engineer.

I currently hold the title of Senior Cyber Security Engineer. Most people don't understand what this position involves. In short, I solve high-value technical information technology problems that protect the people of the United States' Personal Identifiable Information (PII) from domestic and international security threats.

One of the first questions people typically ask who don't understand the field is, "How much money does a Cyber Security Engineer make?" I feel this question is an essential value proposition for young black males of any age if you're trying to get him interested in a STEM career. When I was in high school studying electricity and electronics, and my NFL dreams of grandeur were rapidly fading away, I thought if I could graduate from college and make $35,000, I would be in the words of the great Hip Hop philosopher Rakim, "Paid In Full." Little did I know that the Electronics Engineering Technology Degree I acquired from Norfolk State University would have me earning a six-figure salary by the age of 28.

Like me, most black males are money motivated. It's crucial that we present them with a value proposition of how much money they can earn as motivation when prepping them for STEM careers. Getting an “A” in 8th-grade geometry does not equate to $dollars$ in the mind of a young black male. Studying for a science test is not more important than getting online to play one of your boys in NBA 2k. The latest video from their favorite YouTuber is a way more powerful enticement to waste time than empowering the mind.

I believe that choosing a career path that you are passionate about is more important than doing something for the money. But the primary reason our boys are wasting time trying to be athletes, rappers, entertainers and drug dealers ***is for the money***.

But if we present a value proposition to black boys at a very young age—the salaries they would earn in a STEM career and the purchasing power and status they'd have—you'd have a much more interested, motivated and focused young man on your hands.

I know you think that this tactic is slightly flawed as do I. But the problem we have to take to task is that there is no visibility for the engineer in the black community. The computer scientist doesn't have a popular YouTube channel video of himself getting paid and rolling to the dealership and making it rain on beautiful women. I have not done the research, but we all know very few of us grew up knowing engineers, computer scientists, doctors and lawyers. Those who did were the privileged minority. I didn't grow up knowing any of those professionals.

The NBA and NFL players, rappers, entertainers and even the drug dealers have a more visible platform than the educated professional in the black community. Therefore when we are educating our boys about careers in STEM, we have to embellish a little bit and appeal to the vanity we all have built within us. I was speaking at a career fair for middle school students and was discussing with a group of black boys 12 -14 about going to college and studying engineering and one of the first questions I was asked was, "What kind of car do you drive?" I said, "I drive a 535 BMW XI." His response was, ***"I'm going to be an engineer."***

In the black community, we are still dealing with black boys from different social-economic standings, some of which in 2030 will still be the first members of their families to attend college. Therefore we can't present a message of, do well in math and science in school and you can have a better life because they cannot envision that outcome. One of the reasons that I was prompted to write this book was I get asked by mothers with sons all the time, "How can I get my son into IT, engineering and computer science and can you talk to him?" When I get the opportunity to speak to these young men, I always get a very positive response from the parents, and I know why. One, I leave them with a plan of action. Two, because I am them. There is a negative stereotype of the high tech black male professional, which I don't fit. When I get a chance to speak with boys, they quickly recognize that I am Hip Hop Culture, and they can still be cool, play sports, *and* be themselves *and* be intelligent. The bonus that I tell the older boys that I mentor is, the ladies love a well-educated black man.

The Best Schools Organization provides a listing of the Top 20 Computer and IT Jobs for 2019. You can access this list by navigating to the following website, http://bit.ly/2yWQxl7 which includes…

- Position description
- Median annual salary
- Educational requirements

To search for STEM careers outside of the list provided, do a Google search for Top STEM Careers and Salaries.

Remember, there is nothing wrong with also discussing financial gain when trying to motivate black boys to focus on school and be the best that they can be and maximize their potential. As a parent you want your son to do well in school and go to college for what reasons? I guarantee that one of the main reasons is financial gain, so they can be self-sufficient and get out of your pockets. Do me a favor and list three reasons why you want your son to do well in school. How many of your points lead back to financial gain in some capacity. Since I am 100% sure that this is the case, stop just telling your son to do well in school for the "A," for in his young mind the "A" has no monetary value, but it should stimulate or promote a sense of self-respect.

NOTES

NOTES

Chapter 2: Lessons from My Mother

"A hard head makes for a soft ass."

--Carolyn Elaine Moore

My mother passed away entirely too young at 46 years of age when I was 23. I had just completed my bachelor's degree one year prior. I don't know if my mother had dreams of me going to college growing up, as we never discussed it until I was a senior in high school and was being recruited to play football. But because I was too busy being Hip Hop and defiant to authority in high school, I didn't qualify academically to receive an athletic scholarship. Matter of fact, I graduated high school with a fat 1.69 GPA. That's right, it's not a typo—a "D-" average.

OK, I know you're confused at this point because I stated in the introduction that I virtually tested out of high school with my New York State standardized test scores by the end of 8th grade. But now I'm telling you that I almost failed out of high school. I see the disconnect, and I can feel your confusion as you read this text. I know what you're thinking, "How the hell did he get an engineering degree with those grades?"

Thank God for historically black colleges and universities. Fortunately, I was able to enroll at Norfolk State University, which had an open enrollment policy. It was there where I learned the camaraderie of studying with other young black men aspiring to become professionals. It was there where I would be mentored by well-educated black male professors who pushed me to excellence. But it was the strong educational foundation that I owe to my mother who propelled me to become a successful engineering student.

My mother was a high school graduate and not an educator, but somehow she knew the secret to what people are paying thousands of dollars to programs like Kumon, Huntington, and Sylvan Learning Centers. The best thing that my mother ever did for me educationally was to purchase tons of workbooks: math, science, phonics, connect the dots and coloring books. I would devour them. The problem with education today is they keep trying to reinvent the wheel. There is only one way to get good at something and that is repetition. Alert, alert there is only one way to get good at something, and it's called ***repetition***.

From kindergarten through 5th grade, I had probably completed hundreds of math workbooks and connect the dots. Looking back, this is where I developed the brain for engineering and STEM. As a child math was like a sport to me and I wanted to see how fast I could go. I remember my mother bringing home a math workbook, and I killed it in like 30 minutes. I asked her for another one, and she asked, "What happened to the one I just gave you?" I said, "I completed it." Because I would complete workbooks so quickly, this forced my mother to get smarter, and she began to purchase books beyond my grade level; I would figure those out and destroy those too. My mother never really checked to see if I was doing them correctly, maybe keeping me occupied was enough. But one day my aunt Kathy who worked for the city school district was at my house. My mother asked my aunt to look at the work I was doing in the workbooks because she thought that it was impossible for them to be correct since I was completing them so rapidly. My aunt reviewed a few of the math workbooks and told my mother everything was right in all the books. The reason I remember this is because to reward me, she took me out for ice cream without my older sister. I loved my aunt Kathy.

I wasn't as keen on the phonics and coloring workbooks, but I had to complete them to get more math workbooks. Completing all of the phonics books helped me become an excellent reader by 3rd grade. I remember going to the 6th-grade class for the reading group, and I was placed in the highest level group. One would think that this would be a good thing, and it was for me educationally, but socially, not so much because in today's terms, I developed my first "haters."

See I was the kid who would shout out the answers to all of the questions. I would raise my hand and shout out the answer, whether I was asked or not. When I would go to the upper grades and pull that in the reading group, the girls would suck their teeth, and the older boys that you would call bullies today would give me a few blows to the chest at recess. I thank them for teaching me toughness. Because I was not going to stop raising my hand to read the next paragraph, I had to endure some punishment, but because I was such a good reader at that point, I liked to show off. I also credit the older boys for making me a good football player. Because in 3rd grade, I also made the connection that if I was good at football and other sports, that would overshadow the fact that I was smart.

This is where many of our black boys go wrong. Being smart is looked at as a sign of weakness. Over time I think that we are beginning to dispel this myth, but I still see it in the boys that I coach. My mother would always say, "Boy, you too smart for your own good, but don't think you too smart for a spanking." I was very witty as a young boy, but my mother would always check me if I was getting out of pocket. There was a level of respect she demanded.

Around 5th grade was when I got too cool for workbooks and moved on to my video game phase. I don't remember ever having a conversation with my mother about not doing workbooks anymore, probably because I was an “A+” student until I reached 7th grade. Everything my mother had done before 7th grade had laid a foundation for my success and becoming an engineer. Because from 7th grade on, my grades were less than stellar. I did just enough to pass to the next grade level.

Once I got to 7th grade, I was really feeling myself and began to act out, testing my manhood and fighting in school, being insubordinate to teachers and trying to find my way. I am so grateful for my mother in that every time I was in trouble in school, she would always come to school and was on my side. She would discipline me when we were one-on-one, but she never sided with any of the school officials anytime she had to come to school. Having had the opportunity to be on the other side as a teacher, this wasn't a good practice as it let me know there was nothing the school could do to me. Not that my mother wasn't strict; she was pretty masterful with the belt. But growing up where I lived, some of the stuff I got into was worth a potential whoopin'.

I remember my mother came to an 8th grade open house and I had like a “D” in science. The teacher was going over the grade book with my mother, explaining why I was receiving a “D” for my grade. He stated to my mother that I was at the top of the class with my test scores. "So why is he getting a "D?" she asked. “Well, he never turns in the homework, and a lot of the classwork is incomplete.” My mother looked at me like, *You know you in trouble,* but turned back to the teacher and said, "Well if the purpose of the classwork and homework is to prepare for the test and he passes all of the tests, why are the other assignments weighted so heavily?” She knew exactly why, but she was working for me. He bumped my grade up to a “C.” Knowing that my mom had my back made me appreciate her and try to do better. But I'd succumb to peer pressure after a while.

My mother would ask me, "Why can't you play along with the teachers and do the work?" My mother worked full time before she made it home to cook, I would be headed off to football or basketball practice. Sometimes when I got home from practice she would ask for homework, and I would do it for a little while but then go back to my shenanigans. Having five children myself, I know checking homework is not always a priority, and my children have pulled the wool our eyes plenty of times.

In my opinion, today we face several roadblocks concerning why black males are not achieving in the classroom. First, I believe we are relying too heavily on the school system to educate our sons. Honestly, I don't think that our school systems have a vested interest in the success of black boys. I would say the major reason I have been successful today is because of what my mother did up to the fifth grade. The reason being, though I went to the same schools as my friends that I grew up with, I am the only engineer, and only a small percentage of us were able to go on and complete college.

Dr. Jawanza Kunjufu, whom I would consider an expert in this field, wrote a book that every black mother should read titled, *Countering the Conspiracy to Destroy Black Boys*. This book details the concept of the "4th Grade Failure Syndrome." In short, he describes that black boys are very eager to learn and do exceptionally well up to the 4th grade. After 4th grade, there is a sharp decline in the academic progress of black boys.

NOTES

NOTES

Chapter 3: Quotes from My Father

"Do as I say, not as I do."

--Gerald John Henry Moore

My father was born the middle child of 12, and his parents died before he was a teenager. His story is one of struggle and perseverance. By no means was my dad perfect, but there is not another man that I admire and respect more. As I would often hear the quote above while he was drinking beer, smoking weed or both, I understood or rather I had a healthy fear of what he would do to me if I pushed my boundary. As a young man growing up, this healthy fear of my father prevented me from even trying drugs or alcohol.

However, considering how much most little boys want to be like the men closest to them, or in the absence of a positive male figure, the professional athlete, rapper, entertainer or worse yet, the drug dealer becomes that model of manhood. My father's quote was powerful for me; however flawed, for so many of our young black males ruin their lives because they want to emulate what their idea of manhood is by drinking alcohol, smoking weed and other drugs, and abusing women. Not understanding that all of these ills are gateways to becoming addicts and not being able to become productive men in society.

Sometimes as an adult man it's embarrassing when my friends or colleagues ask, "Gerald, what you drinkin'?" and I hear the voice of my father saying, "Do as I say, not as I do." Therefore, I don't drink alcohol or smoke as my father's message is well-engrained in my psyche.

"You can't make money if you can't do multiple things."

When I was a little boy, my father was always working on something. Although he had to drop out of high school, I remember watching him reading and learning how to build things. In my eyes, he could do anything, from building a car with his bare hands to planting a garden on the side of the house with collard greens, cabbage, peas, tomatoes, squash, even watermelon and that's impressive in the inner city of Rochester, New York, but my father was a country boy from Georgia.

He had his primary job as a machinist, but he also had three or four side hustles. He loved doing autobody work and turned our garage into his shop. I hated this shop, for by the time I was six or seven years old, he had me working in the shop. I appreciate this now, but I used to cry, and my mother would try and bail me out saying the work was too hard. But my father would say in a forceful voice, "Carolyn, this boy needs to learn how to work."

If you ask anyone who knows me well about what I do, they'll probably retort with, "What doesn't he do?" I owe my work ethic and ability to master multiple skills to my father and a few of my uncles. They were builders, and black boys need to see black men building.

Black boys need to have positive black men in their lives; unfortunately, a disproportionate number of black boys are growing up without any positive black male role models that they can touch and feel. Telling a black boy he can be president like Barack Obama is too vague since most parents don't even know someone running for city council in their own city.

“Have respect for yourself and others.”

My father commanded respect and told me at a very young age to have respect for myself. He taught me that if I wasn't going to take pride in what I was doing, then I shouldn’t do it. He said to me that the amount of money I made would be directly connected to my appearance. My father’s work and business was a dirty job, but he loved to get dressed up.

He taught me that looking a man in the eye when speaking to him is the only way to get him to respect you. I remember one time my mother was yelling at me for acting out and he punched me in the chest so quick and so hard, I still feel it to this day. He said, "Respect your mother."

Today you can walk down any street where there is a group of black boys, and you can immediately tell the ones that don't have respect for themselves because their pants will be sagging below their butts. My mother could have done an excellent job of teaching me to have respect for myself and others, and she definitely has implanted some gems in me, but getting that lesson from my father was probably was a lifesaver for me.

"That's a man's job."

Taking out the trash was my job. Getting the groceries out of the car was my job. Cleaning all of the dog poop out of the back yard was my job. Mowing the lawn was my job. Shoveling 15 to 20 inches of snow during the harsh winters of upstate New York was my job. I remember saying to my father, “Why can't my sisters help to shovel snow?” His reply, "That's a man's job." I said, "Well why do I have to do dishes sometimes?" He said, "Because that's a man's job too if you are out on your own."

My father would pay me for a job well done when I was in elementary school. If I did a crap job, he wouldn't pay me, and when I would redo the job correctly and ask for money, he would say, “No, you should have done it right the first time. He taught me to work until completion and have respect for my work product, which has been an invaluable lesson in my professional life. It also taught me to do a hard day’s work for a hard day’s pay.

I find it astounding when I see mothers with their sons at the grocery store, and able-bodied boys are watching their moms load up the car. I see moms mowing the lawn while their teenage son is in the house playing video games. When I see a young woman with a man at the gas station and the woman is pumping the gas with the man in the passenger seat, this disturbs me. Even worse when the man is in the driver seat, and the woman is pumping the gas. Nevertheless, these are the things I learned from my father.

"It's not the school's responsibility to educate our children, because how do they know what they're good at?"

My father said this quote to my mother after one of my middle school suspension meetings. My father had an understanding that my grades in middle and high school were not life-threatening as he had to drop out of school in the 9th or 10th grade, and most of what he knew was self-taught. He also knew that I was smart because I worked with him all the time and being from a blue-collar city, he knew that I would work. They also couldn't pay me for good grades once I got to middle school because I was the paperboy from 12 to 16 years old and was already "Getting My $Bag."

Most people think it's the public school's responsibility to educate their children. This is where they are wrong. The school's responsibility is to deliver state-mandated material to students so that they can pass a series of competencies to maintain state funding. The state's only goal for this type of education is to certify students are competent to enter the workforce at a base level.

This is where I fell victim to the public school system, that was not equipped to deal with a student like me. I was a high achiever on my standardized tests, which said that I had achieved proficient scores in reading and math to complete high school by the end of 8th grade, yet I was still being force-fed the state-mandated programming. Learning about how Christopher Columbus discovered America, **Not,** by teachers who didn't look like me, who took every intellectual challenge that I presented to label me a troublemaker.

In 10th grade, the Social Studies teacher got extremely angry with me for whispering while he was going over notes for a test that we were having the next day and kicked me out of class. The next day we took the test, and I scored the highest in the class, and he accused me of cheating. Mind you, I had a “D” average in the class, primarily because I didn't do the homework.

Before the next chapter test, I got kicked out of class again and was told not to come back until I had a note from the Dean of Students. Which was cool with me, I just took an additional lunch period. When classmates informed me that the chapter test was on Friday, I got a note and showed up for class. Frustrated that I was in the room, he forced me to take the test sitting right next to his desk.

When the test scores came in, he was pissed at me again because his "Prize asshole" student, as he called me once, broke the curve. This means the average scores were so low that he was going to give additional points to the highest grade in the class. That person gets 100% and the difference added to the high grade is also applied to the rest of the class, in an effort to boost letter grades. But because I scored 95% and the average score was like 65%, he could only give an additional 5 points, and a good percentage of the class still failed the test.

The lesson here is that as parents we need to know what our boys are capable of. My father was correct in his quote and most public schools are not equipped to deal with the individual needs of the student. Even though I went to a vocational high school and was learning a trade, I felt like most of my other state-mandated programming was a waste of time.

What if once a student becomes proficient with the state requirement, the school could find out what the student is interested in and place them on that track. I would have wanted to learn about entrepreneurship and money. This is where the public school system falls short for boys that are intelligent, quickly become disengaged and usually get labeled special needs. Unfortunately, this happens around the 3rd or 4th grade, and they never make it through high school at all. Therefore, you cannot be totally dependent on any school system to be the sole or primary educator of your son.

NOTES

NOTES

Chapter 4: Sports and Self Discipline

"Every act of self-discipline in one area of your life will strengthen and reinforce all other areas." --Brian Tracy

One of the hardest most important lessons that we as parents need to teach our children is self-discipline. The reason this is the hardest lesson to teach is that most of us don't have self-discipline ourselves. With the ever-growing number of distractions that we have in our digital world today, developing self-discipline is not an easy thing to do. We all struggle as adults in one area or another with our self-discipline, whether it be managing our time, managing our weight or managing our money.

The definition of self-discipline that I employ for myself and my children is *Do what you are supposed to do when you are supposed to do it, No Matter What.*

When my mother introduced me to math workbooks, I am sure she didn't know she was working on my self-discipline. Because I loved math, I would get a workbook and complete the entire book in one sitting. I couldn't stop until I completed the entire book. Because I did this consistently at such a young age it disciplined and conditioned me to always want to work to completion.

I was about six or seven when I developed my passion for sports, primarily football and basketball, but I played all sports. I wanted to pass the football as a quarterback; I would find someone to play catch with and throw the football over, over and over again until I could throw it to the point where I exceeded my own expectations. I wanted to learn how to dribble a basketball and do fancy dribble moves; therefore, I dribbled the ball in my back yard or up and down the street for hours. Whatever sport I participated in, I would practice the skills until I achieved mastery. Knowing what I know now, I'm sure the self-discipline learned while working on those math workbooks had seeped into the other disciplines of my life to the point where I had to do everything until I gained mastery.

Unfortunately, all boys' minds don't work that way, or as parents we've missed that window and we have to start at a different stage. The good news is self-discipline can be developed at any age. This is where sports come in. I believe that all black boys should be involved in sports in some capacity as early as they can participate. Whether it be team sports like soccer, football, and basketball or individual sports like martial arts, swimming, or track and field.

There are three ways I think that sports improve the over-all self-discipline for black boys.

1. In team sports boys learn that they have to be accountable for the role they play in order for the team to be successful. When I started playing Pop Warner football at age seven, something amazing happened. I developed the spirit to compete and wanted to do and be my very best for the team. The daily ritual of practice, learning and running the plays to perfection made me more disciplined, knowing that if I missed my assignment I would be letting the team down for that one play. This motivated me and taught me how to focus, regardless of the conditions around me. More than anything I learned the self-discipline to show up every day and be focused on the task at hand.

   I also took martial arts as a kid and participated in swimming. Individual sports are amazing to teach self-discipline. When you are training and competing in individual sports, you learn very quickly that you can't depend on anyone else; mommy and daddy can't help you. Unfortunately, as a black male engineer, many of the meeting rooms I step into have no familiar faces that look like me. But it's the self-discipline and mental fortitude that I learned from individual sports that makes me comfortable and able to compete and present my best self.

2. Because all sports build positive work habits, they innately foster self-discipline. Most boys want to play and will work hard in order to do so. I had a coach in high school say to me one day, "There is no one who works harder than you on the court. Why don't you display those habits in the classroom?" I don't believe he really wanted an answer as much as to give me the opportunity to reflect on why I didn't perform in the classroom. I thought about this for years, and the reason my work habits were so much greater on the playing field was that I knew that the other boys on the team depended on and cared about me and I wasn't going to let them down. That feeling of camaraderie I can't compare to anything. The majority of my teachers didn't

look like me, as a matter of fact, I never had a black male teacher in elementary, middle or high school. But when I got to college and I walked into that first technology class and Dr. Cropper told us that he was going to work us hard and we had to be twice as good as a white engineer to be successful, it was the work habits and self-discipline garnered from sports that allowed me to rise to the occasion when that 1.69 GPA from high school said I was destined to be a loser.

3. Complex mathematics happen in real-time in sports. Most of the athletes who are really good at sports—the ones that are not 12 playing with 9-year-olds—are solving a lot of complex equations while they play. Have you ever gone to a football game and watched a running back make a move and get through two would-be tacklers? Well I have done it myself on a regular basis and there was a science to it. In real-time I could calculate the speed at which I was moving, the speed and angle with which the defenders were approaching and at the right moment, split the defenders and cause them to collide. That's calculus and rate of change.

Sports is math. Take an athlete like Allen Iverson, who despite his stature, was dominant in a league of giants. Not only was he a league leader in scoring, but he was also a league leader in steals, which was an even greater feat because it required him to perform much more complex calculations than to simply have the ball in his hands and go to the basket. If someone could have gotten to him as a boy and showed him how he could have also leveraged his gift to be able to make the complex vector analysis he performed night in and night out in real-time on the court, he easily could have been a Ph.D. Physicist.

Sports can play a huge role in developing black boys, especially when they have good coaches. Because of my engineering background, I would often stop practice and relate the mathematics that were happening as we would run a play. I would discuss how to make cuts at the proper angle and use mathematical terms that I knew the boys were using in school. I had a parent one day come up to me in practice and say, “Please continue to use the math terms you are using in practice.” I asked why and she stated that her son was struggling with angles and mathematic theory, but because I was talking about it and how it related to basketball, he had scored 100% on the test when he had failed the quiz two days prior. Not every coach is going to do that, but know those relationships between math and sports are present and most boys are picking it up subconsciously.

NOTES

NOTES

Chapter 5: White Teachers and Self Confidence

"One important key to success is self-confidence. An important key to self-confidence is preparation."

--Arthur Ashe

Self-confidence and self-discipline go hand in hand. I started playing full contact football at eight years old for the Rochester Rams. It was here where awesome men/coaches/mentors poured into me that self-confidence and swagger that I carry with me today.

The younger kids in Pop Warner at the time were called the Jr. Pee Wee division. With this age group, the coaches could actually be on the field and in the huddle with the team. I'll never forget head coach Mr. Carl Whitehead (RIP) said, "Nope, that's not how we gonna do it." Looking back as a little boy I remember the coaching staff pushed us hard; it was almost military. I was the quarterback and in charge of the whole operation. Coach Carl stressed to me and the team that we needed to execute and that the eleven guys on the field needed to work as one and have one voice. We had a cadence that all of our teams said when we got to the line of scrimmage. I would shout, "Rams Ready?" and the team would shout back, "Yeah," and I would look at the other team on defense and I could see the fear in their eyes. We would run up and down the field, and coaches would be on the sidelines laughing while the other coaches were trying to get their boys in the right position. This gave us extreme self-confidence and as little boys we felt proud we did not have our coaches on the field.

Who's instilling that self-confidence into black boys in the public school system? Though I had great coaches and mentors in my life as you've read, I still strayed. But Proverbs 22:6 says, "Train up a child in the way he should go, even when he is old he will not depart from it" [New American Standard Bible (NASB). I still had in me that self-confidence and self-discipline I needed to get myself back on track.

When I talk to young boys in elementary and middle school, I notice their voices are subdued; they won't look into my eyes as I am talking to them. They have no self-confidence in their ability to read and do math. Many of our young black boys are either on medication or being prescribed medication to calm them down, robbing them of their greatness and the fact that they have tons of creative energy. Highly energetic boys are labeled bad and are being recommended for special education. Think about what that does to a young boy's self-confidence to be placed in special education just because he is energetic and enthusiastic.

I taught Technology at Frederick Douglas Middle School in Rochester, New York, which 90% of the student population is economically disadvantaged. I had five classes of seventh and eighth graders, about 125 students. Four of those classes were labeled special education classes and I was instructed to not let any of those kids use any of the equipment. What does this do to a young boy's self-confidence to know that he can't use any of the equipment because he has been labeled not capable of being able to handle basic tools? This group of kids had run the previous white male instructor out of the school with a nervous breakdown. Another teacher was hired, and they ran him out of school in 2 days. Now of course if the kids are unruly and disrespectful you can't have them getting injured in the technology shop. But who is really the problem, the student or the teacher? Nevertheless, I knew that I was going to be successful with this group.

As a new technology instructor, I had to have a mentor or lead teacher whose role would have been to coach and give me pointers on how to deliver instruction. In this specific case his role was going to be teaching me how to babysit a bunch of kids that had run out 4 white male teachers in the last year. Prior to getting my assignment, at which time I would be left alone in the classroom with the students, I had to observe my mentor teacher. After watching his class for 2 days, and these were allegedly the good kids, I went to Mr. Alexander, the principal and told him that my 25-year veteran, seasoned mentor teacher was not qualified to mentor me. Mr. Alexander, a black man, laughed and said, “I know, what do you suggest?” I suggested that he be out of the room for 2 weeks to give me full autonomy to implement the technology curriculum that I had developed. Mr. Alexander agreed.

In that 2-week period I had every class working on projects independently using the equipment in the room. I had separated the boys from the girls and given them individualized instruction as the boys needed to hear a different message than that of the girls. The immediate improvement in self-confidence in the boys was so apparent that teachers from other subjects would come and ask me what I was doing, as boys they could never reach were now coming into class, sitting down, and raising their hands to ask and answer questions. The math teacher had asked one of my students what was up with the sudden change in his behavior. He stated to the math teacher, "Coach Moore is going to be checking in on my other classes and I'm going to have to deal with him if my report is bad."

See I never called myself a teacher because young black boys have adversarial relationships with their teachers as I did. Understand this, the word teacher is synonymous with the word "snitch" in a black boy's mind and we all know what happens to snitches in the hood. The teacher is the one reporting negatively to the boy's administrator, principal and parents. This is a very unfortunate situation that needs to be remedied in our inner-city schools, but we don't have enough community presence in our inner-city schools who can command a level of respect that frankly the majority of white teachers can't attain.

But in contrast I would have run through a brick wall for Coach Carl, and most boys have a higher level of respect for their coaches than their teachers. Boys know the coach is on the same team and they are in this together to win even when they have to get disciplined. I understood as a 24-year-old instructor what my role had to be in those boys' lives that no white man or white woman could deliver. I was delivering a message of love, building self-esteem and confidence from a position that they were familiar with. I also grew up in that neighborhood and could relate to the students on another level. This is no disrespect to white teachers in the way they relate to black boys because there are plenty of white teachers who are awesome at what they do, but at the same time those teachers are few and far between.

As parents we have to make sure that our sons' teachers are not killing their self-confidence. My parents did an awesome job of making sure that my confidence was high by being supportive and on my side, especially when it came to school issues. As many times as I got in trouble, I was never disciplined in front of the school staff. Though I was still acting out, hell, I was a little boy trying to find myself, but what my parents' support did for me allowed me to mature and maintain my self-confidence because I knew they had my back. It's really hard when you have a rambunctious young son, but you can never allow his spirit to be broken.

I believe that if a black boy's self-confidence to read is destroyed in the early stages of development in the 2nd and 3rd grades, he will never be able to catch up. This has been documented as across the country, black boys consistently score low on reading assessments. Therefore, the parents have to make sure that boys are reading at home and not just playing video games.

I had a conversation with a young white female teacher who I asked to be very candid with me about her thoughts and experiences on teaching black boys. I have no doubt that this particular teacher is passionate about teaching. What she stated to me was something that I already knew but getting the confirmation was what I was after. She stated to me that teaching black boys at the younger ages, kindergarten to 2nd grade, was more preferable to her because in her words, "They're so cute." I replied, "Kind of like pets, huh?" She caught herself on her reply, but the smile on her face was the answer. Then she stated that a lot of the teachers she works with become fearful of the boys starting at 4th grade through 8th grade as boys start maturing and some are bigger than their teachers by 6th grade. See the real problem is not the intentions of white teachers but their inherent subconscious bias of black men in the stereotypical portrayal in the news and media. Our boys are being looked at as criminals as early as 4th grade and even in the suburban districts this bias exists.

I have had several conversations with parents with bi-racial boys either with a white mother, black father or vice-versa, and it gets really interesting when the white moms know that their sons are being treated unfairly and the words that are being spoken by teachers when they don't know she has a black son. This commentary is not meant to bash the white teacher, it's just to be informative so that we know what we are dealing with when it comes to black boys who are being taught by white teachers. We need to ensure our boys are in learning environments that will not be detrimental to their development.

NOTES

NOTES

Chapter 6: Video Game Therapy

"You cannot expect to achieve new goals or move beyond your present circumstances unless you change."

--Les Brown

I played video games as a kid and I played a lot. But if I had the choice of playing video games, or going outside and playing sports with my friends or riding my bike, the video games could wait. This is the disconnect that we are having with young boys today who would rather stay glued to mobile devices and gaming consoles. I understand, for in the wintertime in Upstate New York when it was 13 degrees Fahrenheit and -10 degrees wind chill factor outside, it was always a great time to lock in and try to conquer that next level where I kept getting killed.

Atari was the big gaming console when I was coming up. I am really dating myself here. I had just gotten the new Donkey Kong game; I was about 10 years old. I clearly remember it was a Saturday morning; I had begged my mother to take me to the store to get the game as I had saved my birthday money and had just enough. Soon as I got home, I burst into the house loaded it up and the music started playing. *Whoa…* I was instantly engaged.

Level one I'm jumping barrels, climbing ladders trying to save my dearest Pauline, the name of the damsel in distress I had to save from a crazed gorilla. I get to the top alive and Donkey Kong runs off with Pauline and I start the process again on level 2. Twelve hours later I am still locked in. I've turned into a little Italian man named Mario with a big nose and in my mind, I was in the game and I could not detach. Until my father grabbed me by the pants hoisted me in the air and began to spank me.

I don't really know what happened, but legend has it that I told my father to wait as I was trying to clear the level, and being a man of few words when I was in defiance, he handled his business accordingly. Though I scurried up to bed, I was up at daylight the next morning and took another spanking because I refused to get ready for church. Parents can't be afraid to discipline black boys. We all know Proverbs

13:24, “He who withholds his rod hates his son, But he who loves him disciplines him diligently” (NASB).

The 8-bit technology of the Atari gaming console that had me in such a trance is nothing compared to the 64- and 128-bit Xbox and PlayStation systems with high definition and realistic 3D worlds the kids are playing today. These games are deliberately designed, with the help of psychologists, to make players want to keep playing. And we as parents are subjecting our children at younger and younger ages to more and sophisticated and virtual reality games that their young minds are not equipped to know the difference between what’s fake and what’s real.

Our black boys tend to be more susceptible to being addicted to video games, which some parents are using as pacifiers. Psychologists are now treating children with gaming addictions and seeing a correlation between excessive gaming and traits associated with attention deficit disorder, anxiety, depression and autism.

Researchers have documented that video games have been shown to increase dopamine levels by 100%. Dopamine levels are associated with the reward center of the brain. When we sense something pleasurable, our dopamine levels increase. It's nature's way of reinforcing behaviors that are often necessary for survival. But this is also why boys are becoming addicted to video games.

As this book is not going to take a deep dive into the chemical effects video games have on a developing boy's emotions, in addition to dopamine I would suggest parents google the effects of oxytocin, endorphins and serotonin while gaming, as these chemicals in the body elicit emotions that may be erratic for your son.

Video game play is not the only culprit as parents are arming children as young as 3 years old with mobile phones, tablets and other digital devices. On one hand this may seem like a good idea if a child is using them for educational purposes, but are we setting the child up to become emotionally dependent on a mobile device.

I have two sons who are 15 years apart in age. My older son grew up as a gamer and hell, I played with him. I was a fan of sports games like Madden and NBA 2K. My older son did not own a tablet and did not have a cell phone until high school, and the phone was not a smart phone. Of course, my younger son was armed with a tablet at 5, a mobile phone at 11 and now we are in damage repair mode at 14.

The initial thought was to get the tablet for educational purposes and reading books. I remember when I got the tablet and loaded it with well over 30 books. Awesome on a long ride in the car, he'd read and do math, maybe learn some science. Then that turned into him begging for games and moving further and further away from the educational piece. Then came the smartphone and the begging for Instagram, Snapchat and gaming apps and worse yet, YouTube. My son loves watching YouTube videos because he is a basketball fan, and I must admit that YouTube is an incredible medium for amateur basketball highlights. My younger son is a twin and his sister also loves YouTube, but the difference is the content she watches actually has language being spoken, while he's watching basketball highlights.

One day I called my son from his room; I asked him a question and he literally grunted at me. I thought I was tripping a little bit, so I asked him again and he kind of shrugged his shoulders and made some primitive sound. I knew immediately what was happening, and I snatched the phone from his hand and told him he was done. I was thinking to myself, He's really regressing to a caveman status. He was not allowed to have the phone back for a week. That very next morning he was back to himself. I really believe that he was entranced and in the YouTube version of the movie "The Matrix." Prior to giving him the phone back, I disabled all the apps on the phone. Once he got it back and realized that all of the apps were disabled, he didn't even want to carry the phone. I reinforced to him that the phone is for his mother and me to contact him, not for mobile entertainment. But I struck a deal with him that I would allow him to use apps for an hour a day, which you can program on the iPhone.

Truly I don't think that video games are bad in moderation. There are some really good games that actually enhance your critical thinking skills, creativity, reflexes and cooperation. But endless hours of video game play are not good for anyone, and I have several stories that parents have told me similar to my son's experience.

I would suggest to parents to monitor the video game play of their boys. Especially boys under the age of 12. Even if you believe that you have control of the tablet or the smartphone, and your son is using it for educational purposes, the problem that schools are having now is that children cannot write or do written math equations. I would suggest for every hour of smartphone or tablet time that you incorporate written work and reading from real books where you have to flip the pages. Now that many of our schools are doing more with computers and tablets it's very important that we reinforce reading books and writing. This is a real world that we live in and not a digital one. Video games and mobile devices should still be considered a privilege not a constitutional right.

NOTES

NOTES

Chapter 7: What is Education for Black Boys?

"Education is the most powerful weapon which you can use to change the world."
--Nelson Mandela

It is not to be challenged and I believe we have a consensus on the quote from Nelson Mandela above that education is the most powerful weapon to be used to change the world. But the challenge is how do we translate that message to a young black boy whose mother works day and night, there's no father in the home, he hates his teachers, he's having no success in school and the only reason he's still attending is because he can get two meals a day?

In all reality this book may not reach that mother who is doing her best to raise her black son, working 16-hour days just to make ends meet. But it may reach a neighbor, aunt, uncle, cousin, camp counselor, basketball coach or random stranger. These are the people who were my extended school system. What we are lacking today is the humanity to take an interest in and support those young black boys standing right before us who are just like I was. But for the grace of God, I am able to write this book as there were many instances as a young man and boy where I placed myself in situations that I am fortunate to have escaped with my life because of the wisdom and caring of others.

I have great memories of those persons who interceded and gave me educational lessons in life with love. What black boys are lacking are those individuals willing to step in and fill a void and inject hugs and smiles into their lives instead of dissension and punishment.

"I believe that education is all about being excited about something. Seeing passion and enthusiasm helps push an educational message."

--Steve Irwin

I get excited when I meet teachers who are enthusiastic and passionate about what they do. I recently visited a private school where I was thinking about enrolling my son. Though the school only had a couple of black boys in each class, I spoke to a few of them and they were happy and excited to be there. Then I went to a couple of the classes; there was high energy, the students were engaged and one of the teachers was so involved with the activity she didn't recognize that I was in the room for 10 minutes until one of the students informed her.

Then there was a hint of sadness because I wondered if the majority of black boys were in highly engaged classrooms with teachers that were passionate about educating them more than medicating them. I wondered if when I walk into meeting rooms there would be young engineers that I could mentor who would ultimately replace me. For in many of the companies I have worked over my 20-year career as an engineer I have not had the pleasure of mentoring young black male professionals year after year. I get a thrill out of sharing my knowledge, wisdom and life experiences, especially with young black boys because many of them are not becoming men.

I recommend parents get to know their sons' teachers, especially in the primary grades. If they do not seem excited and enthused about teaching and you sense that teaching is more a paycheck than a passion, move your son to a new class. For these individuals have an influence on how school and education will be perceived for the rest of his life.

"Don't let schooling interfere with your education."
--Mark Twain

This is such a powerful quote. As I stated in the previous chapter, the majority of public schools are just shoveling state-mandated materials down our children's throats without the intent of teaching them how to learn.

I was 15 years old when I learned the word "autodidact." I was having a conversation with my biology teacher in high school, one of the two black women instructors I had the pleasure of being part of my life. The reason I was having this conversation was that I was failing her class and she was trying to figure out how to reach me because I never came to class, yet I had the highest test average of all of her students.

In this conversation, she was wise enough to ask me what I liked to do. As we were conversing I started talking about electrical circuits and installing car stereos and designing subwoofer boxes for the drug dealers in my neighborhood. Yes, I did tell her my designs were for the drug dealers in the neighborhood. She asked to see my notebook and she was amazed that I was calculating Thiele/Small Parameters, which are electromechanical parameters that define the specified low-frequency performance of a loudspeaker driver. As I was trying to explain to her the concept in layman's terms, that Thiele/Small parameters is how you get that “Boom, Boom, Boom,” she immediately lit up and said, “Mr. Moore, I think you are an autodidact, which means a self-taught person.” See I never took any notes in class and failed notebook check every time and clearly I wasn’t cheating on the test as I scored the highest whether it was open notes or not. She was correct for the most part; I hated my classes, but I did like school and I would teach myself outside of school the things I wanted to learn.

She asked if I would be interested in attending a 2-week summer technology program at Rochester Institute of Technology. I did not qualify for the program as I needed to have a 3.5 grade point average, but she stated that she would make a call to the university and make a special case for me. I did attend the camp and I was the only black boy in the camp. I really felt out of place at the camp and was kind of standoffish. Though it was a great opportunity, I really didn’t embrace it and took every chance I got to be by myself. But what being on the campus did was change my mindset about my ability to attend college.

I also knew at that moment if I was going to attend college, I would prefer that it be a historically black college.

Black boys need to feel like they have a say in their education. I suggest all parents ask their sons often what their interests are and help them to pursue those interests. Give them the opportunity to be active participants in what they are learning. There is currently a paradigm shift being made in high tech corporate America where creativity is beginning to have more value than the degree, especially in the information technology fields as certificates in specialized areas are becoming more and more valuable assets. Because the universities cannot keep up with the speed of technology. The most important educational opportunity you can provide for black boys is exposure to any and everything that they show an interest in.

"Education must not simply teach work—it must teach Life"
--W.E.B. Du Bois

Black boys more than anything need to learn life skills as a major part of the education process, and these life skills are not going to come from school. In the hood, we like to say that someone is street smart, meaning they're not good with the books, but they got a good hustle. Also in the hood, we say someone is book smart, meaning they are highly educated, but lack the common sense that one would gain from real life experiences. Black boys need to be in that sweet spot where they can navigate both of these worlds. I preach to my sons all the time to follow their passion and learn everything there is to know about whatever it is, and if it's a true passion and you believe in it then whatever it is will provide a living for you and your family. We tend to place a lot of emphasis on education and going to college to further that learning without ever trying to figure out what our actual gifting is. Your education is not your gift. I am an engineer and that is my job, but it's not my gift. I'm very fortunate in the fact that my gift and my education work hand in hand. I am a leader of men and my gift is my ability to reach young men and get them to move in a positive direction. This brings me great joy and satisfaction. My job could be gone tomorrow, and my gifting would sustain me. I was blessed with the aptitude to become an engineer and I leverage this with my gift to teach black boys technology.

I believe if we can help black boys find what they are gifted at and build education around that gift, then our boys would be more successful and more enthused about education. For when education is maturing one's gifting, there is another level of passion toward learning. How many of us have degrees in fields we care nothing about? How many of us are our job titles or degree titles and nothing else?

NOTES

NOTES

Chapter 8: Goal Setting, The Secret Sauce to Reaching Black Boys

"A goal properly set is halfway reached."

--Zig Ziglar

Most employed persons have some type of formal performance review by management yearly and this typically determines how much of a raise or bonus you will receive. Sometimes the review is just arbitrary depending on what you do, whether you made it to work on time, how many times you called out or how many widgets you managed to produce for the year.

I have primarily been employed by management consulting firms and most of my yearly performance reviews were based on goals that I set for myself. Typically, these goals are categorized as Corporate Career Goals, Educational Goals and Leadership Goals. Then there were metrics set to ensure that I was working toward achieving the goals that I set for myself, the operative words being, "Goals that I set for myself."

Quarterly there was some type of review to go over the metrics, so there was quality control and someone who would hold me accountable and help me stay on track. At the end of the cycle someone at the upper management level would judge my performance against my goals and metrics and decide if I deserved to receive a raise, bonus, promotion or whatever benefits were tied to my performance review.

In most households we actually have this management consulting performance review style plan in place. Unfortunately, the plan does not come with any goals and is usually based on a fictitious fat white man flying in on reindeer, landing on top of your roof, jumping down a chimney that you may or may not have, deciding whether your child was naughty or nice and rewarding them for a great year and job well done. We call this yearly review Christmas. Think about how ridiculous this sounds in writing. Then six days later January 1st arises and most of us ask our children what their New Year's resolution is without any metrics or checks and balances to ensure success.

This yearly review plan would work great if upper management—yes, you the parent, guardian, teacher and/or role model, who has the child under your supervision, especially black boys—set **Career Goals,**

Educational Goals, and **Leadership Goals**. We can't blame our sons for a lack of structure from upper management or for the fact they have not decided to make a shift from a failing family business model of the Christmas yearly review and reward system.

It's time to update your son's annual performance review plan. Think about what you already have in place: New Year's Day the beginning of the year, and most schools are broken into four quarters, usually 10 weeks, and Christmas at the end of the year. You already have a timeline to check in, review and reward. You even have a built-in bonus reward system at birthdays and summer vacation.

Many parents have made what used to be privileges into entitlements for their sons. I often hear, "My son must have the Jordan's, with the Don Juan Jeans and whatever Italian brand name t-shirt." "My son has the Xbox, so I'm going to get him the PlayStation or the Nintendo Switch." Most often these rewards are not tied to any form of goal-oriented achievement; therefore, eliminating in the minds of their sons the value of setting goals and achieving them.

As a parent these are the things that you are responsible for:

a) Food

b) Shelter

c) Clothing

d) Nurturing, Love

Parents, understand Oreo cookies are not food and are a privilege. Gaming systems and access to those systems are a privilege. Designer clothes are a privilege. Going out to McDonald's, Chick-fil-A or whatever establishment your son has made you believe is a must have and you feel bad if you don't get it, is a privilege and bonus.

Now here is what you must do. It is mandatory for black boys to have structure. They need to learn to set goals under your guidance and be actively working on them. Goals and structure lead back to self-discipline and self-confidence, for when you are rewarded for achieving a goal you feel good about yourself, and it increases your feelings of self-worth.

Many corporations use S.M.A.R.T. goals to manage whether they are meeting objectives for the company and its personnel. I believe this is the perfect system for helping black boys to become more goal oriented and structured. In order to attain a career in a STEM field these traits are a must.

I have created a S.M.A.R.T. goal setting template that you can use for your son in the Chapter 10 Bonus Materials. You can also find the downloadable template here: http://bit.ly/mbb_smart_goals

What is S.M.A.R.T. goal setting? SMART is an acronym that stands for Specific, Measurable, Attainable, Realistic, and Time-Bound.

Specific – A specific goal is detailed to exactly what is it that you want to achieve. The more specific you are, the more likely you are re to succeed. (A specific S.M.A.R.T. goal could be to achieve a higher grade in a class, specifically going from a B to an A.)

Measurable – The goal has some type of metric to determine success. (S.M.A.R.T. goal keeping room clean, which could be measured during a weekly room inspection)

Attainable – An attainable goal has to be realistic based on your son. (S.M.A.R.T. goal going from a D to an A in a class may not be attainable and a more realistic goal of D to C is more attainable, but a D to a B gets an additional reward)

Relevant – the goals need to be relevant to your son. (S.M.A.R.T. goal may be to read more, but reading the bible may not be best way to get him to read. Allowing him to pick a book and incentivizing completion is more relevant.)

Time-Bound – all goals should have a realistic completion date. (S.M.A.R.T. goal to improve grades in school by progress report time, and finalized on the report card date)

I urge you to start setting S.M.A.R.T. goals with your sons. You'll be amazed at how accomplished they'll feel when they achieve a goal that they've written down and gone through a process to succeed. How rewarding is that to you as a parent that you can participate in the process with your son and feel good about rewarding them for a job well done and take all of the credit away from Santa Claus.

It's never a bad time to start setting S.M.A.R.T. goals, but as I recommended above, leverage the dates that most of us already have built into our lives: start of school, end of quarters, progress report time, holidays, birthdays and summer vacation.

NOTES

NOTES

Chapter 9: Game Plan, 5 Steps to the Epiphany

"Epiphanies awaken the soul."

--A.D. Posey

The main purpose of writing this book is to provide parents a framework to help guide and prepare black boys for STEM careers of the future. I am a proponent for black boys and young black males and will always see them from a glass-half-full mentality. Though we are challenged with strife and many barriers, we still rise, and with the right game plan, we will redefine and change the narrative of the young black male. I use the word epiphany to define a manifestation of a divine supernatural being because the development of the black boy into the black man is that crucial to the black community. It is a must for the survival of the black community that we develop technically-skilled black boys into professionally capable black men.

In this chapter I will provide for you my 5-Step Game Plan to the Epiphany.

Step 1. Be Present

Black boys more than anything need love, support, encouragement and understanding. They will not succeed without someone consistently advocating on their behalf. Never ever trust the school system to be the primary educator, public or private. Go back to Chapter 2: Lessons from My Mother, adapt your own home school system to ensure that your son is competent in reading, writing and arithmetic. I also mentioned earlier in this book reading, *Countering the Conspiracy to Destroy Black Boys*, by Dr. Jawanza Kunjufu. This book will give more insight into the data and statistics about black boys and education. Share this information with your sons to motivate them.

Step 2. Goal Setting (S.M.A.R.T.)

Before your son can achieve anything in life, he needs to know what he wants. You must be able to guide him early on to what's important initially based on your expectations and values. But as he matures, he needs to have primary input on his goals with you as the accountability coach, making sure that not only is he working on his goals but is being rewarded upon completion. I discussed setting S.M.A.R.T. goals and how to schedule a yearly plan for review in Chapter 8. I created a template that you can download: http://bit.ly/mbb_smart_goals to assist you to assist you in this endeavor. These S.M.A.R.T. goals should be posted in a visible area and revisited often.

Aside from helping him believe in himself and setting him up for success in school, goal setting will also benefit in many other ways, including

- Improving his self-image
- Increasing awareness of his strengths
- Increasing awareness of his weaknesses
- Providing an experience of success
- Facilitating effective visualization
- Clarifying the path ahead
- Encouraging prioritization
- Defining reality and separating it from wishful thinking
- Developing responsibility
- Improving decision making

Step 3. Self-Discipline

Black boys must develop self-discipline. In Chapter 4 I led with a quote from Brian Tracy, "Every act of self-discipline in one area of your life will strengthen and reinforce all other areas." No matter what type of discipline you use with your son, the ultimate strategy should be to teach self-discipline. One of the reasons that I didn't stray too far off my path was because of the self-discipline that I learned from sports and the words of wisdom I got from my father.

Here are 4 additional things you can do to help your son learn and practice self-discipline:

1) **Provide Structure** – a good daily schedule, morning routine and afterschool routine will teach your son to divide his time between chores, homework and activities. Over time your son will learn to implement the routine without being prompted. These positive habits will have a definite impact on his future.

2) **Establish Consequences** – sometimes natural consequences are the best teacher. Your son leaves his coat at school, but instead of you picking it up for him, he'll have to be cold on his way to school the next day. If homework is incomplete and it's tied to a S.MA.R.T. goal, there will be no reward upon completion of the goal.

3) **Praise Good Behavior** – reward your son for being discipline. If his job is to take out the trash, it should be done without prompting.

If it's done, he should be rewarded depending on his age. It may be a special treat or an allowance for an older boy. But he should not be rewarded when he has not done what was required of him.

4) **Model Self-Discipline** – We all have bad habits that we don't want our children to exhibit. My father's quote in Chapter 3, "Do as I say, not as I do," is a flawed concept and since our sons are always watching, we should strive to be the model of self-discipline that we want them to be. If you watch too much TV or procrastinate doing things that you say you are going to do, they'll pick up on your habits. If you lose your temper and/or are angry all the time, think about the message you are sending. Ask your son to give you reminders when he sees you not displaying self-discipline and make sure he knows that you are trying to do better and you're in this together.

Step 4. Problem-Solving Skills – Problem solving is the foundation of your son's future. Black boys seem to encounter more problems in this society than most other races. Your son's ability to solve problems and think critically may one day save his life. That seems really dire, but I was put in several situations as a teenager where a simple yes or no choice could have landed me in jail or worse. Don't be a helicopter parent; black boys need to be confident and sure of themselves. Allow them to fail, then ask questions that will allow them to solve their own problems. Build in occasional problems for them to solve. Let them in on problems that you are having at work or in some other facet of life and get their input. The best thing that you can do for your son is ask them for help. You will be surprised at how creative he can be if you just ask.

Step 5. Leadership – Leadership is one of the most important traits that your son can learn. As I mentioned in Chapter 4, I believe that all black boys should be involved in some type of team and/or individual sport. This is where leadership is developed. Learning how to win, how to recover from a loss or cope with failure. It will take leadership and the willingness to stand alone to pursue that STEM career and do what's required when everyone else has quit because they think the course load is too hard. Here are 7 ways you can instill leadership skills in your son:

1) **Set a good example.**

   Your role as a parent, guardian or supervising official is to show leadership and accountability.

2) **Build negotiation skills.**

Instead of giving a hard "yes" or "no" to a request, make an offer and allow them to counter.

3) **Practice confident communication.**

A great way to do this is when you go out to a restaurant, allow your son to place his order directly with the server.

4) **Have a family game night.**

Family game night provides a unique way to spend time together, learn to think strategically and promote positive competition.

5) **Find a mentor.**

If your son expresses interest in an area that you are not equipped to teach, find a trusted friend, family member or organization that can help provide information.

6) **Teach planning skills.**

Involve your son in the planning of his life. Have him set a daily calendar of what time he has to get up, what date/time he has activities. If there is a vacation coming up, involve him in the planning.

7) **Encourage reading.**

One of the most powerful abilities that a black boy must possess is the ability to read and read well. If education is the key to success, your ability to read is the key to education. The ability to read and communicate effectively will open all doors.

By implementing these **5 Steps to the Epiphany** with your son, regardless of his age—and the earlier the better—you will ensure his success. He will not only acquire a degree and a job in a STEM field he will also achieve any goal he sets in his life. To assist you on this journey I am going to provide my support by offering a free subscription to the Black Boys Read Book Club and 30-day access to Gerald Moore Online Technology School for Black Boys.

There is a link and a code located in Chapter 10: Bonus Materials you can use to access both programs.

NOTES

NOTES

Chapter 10: Bonus Materials

"I learned that courage was not the absence of fear, but the triumph over it. The brave man is not he who does not feel afraid, but he who conquers that fear."

--Nelson Mandela

Now that you have made it through this book, and you're convinced that black boys need a game plan for success, I want you to know that you are not alone on this journey. Whether you have a two-parent household, you're a single mother, single father or in a leadership position, you know it's tough to raise black boys in America and abroad.

To give this book life I have added Bonus Materials to help support the mission of cultivating black boys into high achievers.

Bonus 1.

Register your email address at www.motivateblackboys.com to receive new and exciting materials right in your inbox.

Bonus 2.

You will have free access to Black Boys Read Book Club. You can use either of the links below to register: https://www.geraldmooretechnologyschoolforblackboys.com/courses/black-boys-read-book-club or short link: http://bit.ly/blackboysread

Bonus 3.

Free 30-day access to Online Technology School for Black Boys is yours by accessing the following link: http://www.gmtsbb.com

Code: MOTIVATE

Bonus 4.

Free download of the S.M.A.R.T. goals worksheet mentioned in Chapter 8 when using the following link: http://bit.ly/mbb_smart_goals

Bonus 5.

Motivate Black Boys Closed Facebook Group where we can share ideas and resources.

www.facebook.com/groups/motivateblackboys or short link http://bit.ly/mbbfacebook

Please make sure to follow all of our social media channels where we will be promoting positive edutainment for black boys.

Instagram: @gmtsbb or www.instagram.com/gmtsbb

Facebook: www.facebook.com/gmtsbb

YouTube: http://bit.ly/gmtsbb-youtube

Twitter: https://twitter.com/gmtsbb

To contact me directly, contact motivateblackboys.com. I really want to be interactive with you and it would be awesome if you would share your stories of success and pictures of your boys in action to tribe@motivateblackboys.com. I am grateful for the opportunity to be a resource to support black boys and if you would share this book or purchase another book for someone who could use the information, we can change lives together.

NOTES

NOTES

About the Author

Gerald A. Moore Sr. (Coach Moore) has over 20 years of experience as an engineer and has been dedicated to uplifting and motivating young black males. He is the founder of the Gerald Moore Online Technology School for Black Boys, www.gmtsbb.com, which has a mission to train black boys internationally in Computer Science, Information Technology, Web/Mobile application development and emerging technologies.

As a philanthropist he is the treasurer and board member of the Team Jenny Bean non-profit organization, www.teamjennybean.com, which has a mission to help children with chronic conditions and their families.

Coach Moore has been featured in Black Enterprise Magazine Digital Edition as BE Modern Man of Distinction. Gerald loves to play tennis, engages in fitness training and is an avid world traveler and largemouth bass fisherman.

As a Life Coach and Personal Trainer, Gerald has helped his clients lose weight by helping them develop their mental fitness in order to live healthy lifestyles.

Coach Moore lives in the Washington D.C. Metro area where he works with many youth organizations coaching, speaking and mentoring black boys. Gerald has five children: Gerald Jr, Andrea, Lauren, twins Jada and Jordan, and one grandson Noah.

Motivate Black Boys:

How to Prepare Your Sons for Careers in Science, Technology, Engineering and Mathematics

Gerald A. Moore Sr.

Made in the USA
Las Vegas, NV
28 September 2022